YOUR LAND
AND
MY LAND

We Visit

CUBA

Kathleen

Tracy

Mitchell Lane
PUBLISHERS
P.O. Box 196
Hockessin, Delaware 19707

Brazil

Chile

Colombia

Cuba

Dominican Republic

Mexico

Panama

Puerto Rico

Peru

Venezuela

YOUR LAND
AND
MY LAND

We Visit
CUBA

Printing   1   2   3   4   5   6   7   8   9

Library of Congress Cataloging-in-Publication Data
Tracy, Kathleen.
  We visit Cuba/by Kathleen Tracy.
      p. cm. — (Your land and my land)
  Includes bibliographical references and index.
  ISBN 978-1-58415-890-5 (library bound)
  1. Cuba—Juvenile literature. I. Title.
  F1758.5.T73 2010
  972.91—dc22
                                                          2010006558

PUBLISHER'S NOTE: This story is based on the author's extensive research,
which she believes to be accurate. Documentation of this research is on
page 61.
    The Internet sites referenced herein were active as of the publication date.
Due to the fleeting nature of some web sites, we cannot guarantee they will all

Contents

Introduction

The term *Latin America* has no single definition. It was coined in France in the nineteenth century during the reign of Napoleon III to show the cultural bonds between France and many areas in the New World.

In some cases, the term refers to the countries south of the United States. Other times, it refers to Central and South America and all the Caribbean countries. But most commonly, and for our purposes, it describes the Western Hemisphere countries where Spanish and Portuguese—and to a lesser extent French—are the primary spoken languages. Another way of thinking about Latin American countries is this: They are the countries in the Americas that were once part of either the Spanish or Portuguese empire.

Latin America encompasses a wide geographic area, from the Strait of Magellan at the tip of Argentina to the eastern Caribbean Sea. Although Latin America shares common languages, a common religion (Catholicism), and similar colonial backgrounds, each country has a

The Regions and Countries of Latin America

Caribbean: Cuba, the Dominican Republic, and
    Puerto Rico
North America: Mexico
Central America: Belize, Costa Rica, El Salvador,
    Guatemala, Honduras, Nicaragua, Panama
South America: Argentina, Bolivia, Brazil, Chile,
    Colombia, Ecuador, Guyana, Paraguay, Peru,
    Suriname, Uruguay, Venezuela

unique history and distinctive culture that is the foundation of its
national identity. In this book we'll explore Cuba, a country long
isolated that is now looking to integrate itself into the twenty-first
century.

Built around a natural harbor, Havana is one of the most colorful cities in the Caribbean. Noted for its Colonial Spanish architecture, music clubs, narrow streets, and engaging residents, the historic old town *Habana Vieja* (Colonial Havana) has been named a United Nations Educational, Scientific and Cultural Organization (UNESCO) World Heritage Site.

Country Overview

Welcome to Cuba, called Pearl of the Antilles by the Spanish because it was the largest and most valuable island in the Caribbean.

Located just 90 miles south of Key West, Florida, the Republic of Cuba is an archipelago, or chain of islands, that includes the main island and more than 1,600 smaller islands, cays, and coral reefs. The population of Cuba is mainly of Spanish and African ancestry.

The area of the Caribbean where Cuba is located has many names. Christopher Columbus called it the West Indies, mistakenly believing he had sailed near the coast of India. Later, Spain and France called the islands the Antilles, named after the mythological island of Antilia. The larger islands, which include Cuba, Jamaica, Hispaniola (now Haiti and the Dominican Republic), and Puerto Rico, came to be known as the Greater Antilles. The smaller islands closer to Venezuela became the Lesser Antilles.

For almost two centuries now, Cuban tobacco has been considered the finest in the world. Called *cohiba* by the island's inhabitants, tobacco was used as medicine and in cultural and religious rituals. Europeans prized the plants for smoking. While tobacco was indigenous to Cuba, sugarcane was brought to the island by Europeans and was first planted in 1512. By the late eighteenth century, Cuba was the world's largest sugar producer.

You might be surprised to know the island was a favorite vacation spot for wealthy Americans during the early 1950s. Nicknamed the Latin Las Vegas, visitors stayed at luxurious hotels with casinos run by such infamous American mobsters as Lucky Luciano and Meyer Lansky. Clubs were packed with people who stayed up all night dancing to Cuban music played by local musicians, often not leaving until the sun was coming up. Sunbathers filled the sandy beaches year-round, and restaurants prospered, serving freshly caught fish and side dishes of fried plantains, which are a kind of banana.

After Fidel Castro came to power in 1959, the partying came to an abrupt stop. Castro established a communist dictatorship in Cuba, and because he had close political ties to the Soviet Union, the U.S. government no longer allowed Americans to travel to Cuba. The country became isolated, and while the rest of the world moved from the industrial age to the digital age, the Cuban people were stuck in a kind of cultural time warp. Many of the modern conveniences that

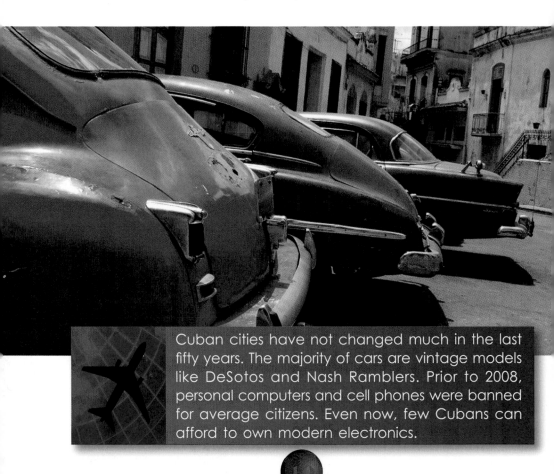

Cuban cities have not changed much in the last fifty years. The majority of cars are vintage models like DeSotos and Nash Ramblers. Prior to 2008, personal computers and cell phones were banned for average citizens. Even now, few Cubans can afford to own modern electronics.

Cuba has over 200 beaches, many of which are considered some of the most beautiful in the world. The main tourist resorts include Jardines del Rey, Cayo Coco, and Cayo Guillermo on the islands along the northern coast.

developed countries came to take for granted, such as cable TV, personal computers, and cell phones, were unavailable in Cuba—and they are still rare on the island. One upside of Cuba's half century of isolation is that the island's natural environment has remained largely untouched. Unlike most other Caribbean islands, the beaches are still free of resort hotels and other signs of civilization. As a result, the island has become a popular eco-tourism destination.

After Barack Obama's election as U.S. president in 2008, and Fidel Castro's retirement that year, the political climate between the United States and Cuba began to change.

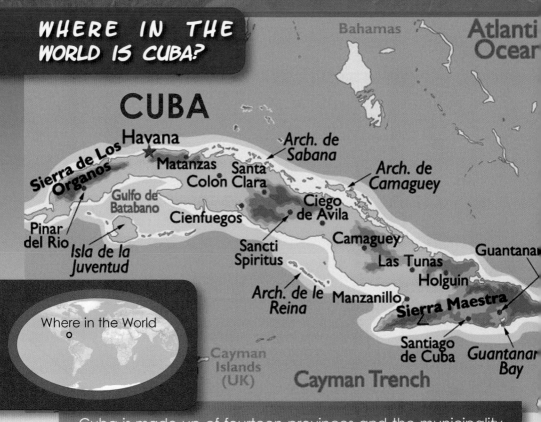

CUBA

Havana
Sierra de Los Organos
Matanzas · Santa Clara · Colón
Arch. de Sabana
Arch. de Camaguey
Gulfo de Batabano
Cienfuegos
Ciego de Ávila
Pinar del Río
Isla de la Juventud
Sancti Spiritus
Camaguey
Las Tunas
Guantanamo
Holguin
Arch. de le Reina
Manzanillo
Sierra Maestra
Santiago de Cuba
Guantanamo Bay
Cayman Islands (UK)
Cayman Trench
Bahamas
Atlantic Ocean

Where in the World

Cuba is made up of fourteen provinces and the municipality of Isla de la Juventud. It is ringed by several smaller archipelagos (labeled Arch.). Pico Real del Turquino, the highest point in Cuba, is the triangle in the Sierra Maestra.

The island is poised to end its longstanding isolation and begin interacting with more of the world. At the same time, Cubans want to protect their country's natural beauty, maintain their unique cultural heritage, and celebrate the island's rich history. In other words, they want to modernize but not necessarily Westernize.

Cuba is a unique destination, offering visitors a vivid step back in time while simultaneously offering modern creature comforts in the few tourist hotels available. It is a country incredibly rich in the arts but stunningly poor. It's an island looking forward to the future but indelibly informed by its past. To get an idea of where Cuba goes from here, it's integral to understand the country's past.

CUBA FACTS AT A GLANCE

Butterfly Jasmine

Full country name: Republic of Cuba
Language: Spanish
Population: Over 11 million
Area: 42,800 square miles (110,860 sq km)
Capital City: Havana (pop. 2.2 million)
Government: Communist State
Ethnic makeup: Spanish (60%), mixed-race (22%), African descent (11%),
   Chinese (1%)
Religion: Catholic (47%), Protestant (4%), Santería (2%)
Climate: Tropical. Warmest month: July (86°F/30°C); Coolest: January
   (70°F/21°C)
Average yearly rainfall: 52 inches (132 cm)
Highest Point: Pico Real del Turquino (6,476 ft/1,974 meters)
Longest River: Cauto (229 miles/369 km)

Flag: The Cuban flag was designed in 1850 by nationals wanting independence from Spain. The three blue stripes represent the divisions of the island at the time; the white stripes symbolize justice. The triangle represents freedom, equality, and brotherhood; it is red for the blood shed during the fight for independence. The star represents absolute freedom of the Cuban people.

National flower: The butterfly jasmine, which represents purity, rebelliousness, and independence. It grows in the wild along riverbanks and lagoons but is also a popular garden flower that thrives in the island's humid climate.

National bird: The tocororo, or Cuban trogon. Its colorful red-white-and-blue plumage matches the colors of the flag.

National tree: Royal palm. This sturdy tropical tree is able to withstand hurricane winds.

FYI FACT:

Robert Louis Stevenson's *Treasure Island* and James M. Barrie's *Peter Pan* were partly inspired by written accounts of Isla de la Juventud's pirate history.

Santiago de Cuba was founded in 1514 by explorer Diego Velázquez. Located on the southeast end of the island, Santiago is Cuba's second largest city and is known for being the home of many famous Cuban musicians.

Brief History

Cuba was first settled around 3,000 years ago by a South American tribe called the Ciboney. Later, the island was occupied by another South American people called the Taíno, believed to have come from Venezuela. A bellicose tribe, the Taíno took over most of the island, and by the time Christopher Columbus arrived in 1492, the remaining Ciboney were found only in a small area on the western side of the island.

The Taíno lived in small villages throughout the island and grew a variety of crops, including peanuts, maize, beans, squash, and yucca. They also grew tobacco, which would become a highly prized crop by Europeans.

Santiago de Cuba was designated a Spanish colony in 1514 by explorer and conquistador Diego Velázquez, who arrived on the island with 300 soldiers. Other explorers used Santiago as a jumping-off point for expeditions. Hernán Cortés and Hernando de Soto embarked from Santiago to explore Mexico and Florida, respectively. Santiago was the capital of Cuba from 1522 until 1589, when Havana was named the capital city.

Velázquez established seven European settlements that used the local Indians for what amounted to slave labor. Many Taíno committed suicide, preferring death to losing their freedom. The Taíno chief, named Hatuey, was executed for refusing to convert to Catholicism. The remaining Taíno either died from starvation, were killed at the hands of the colonists, or succumbed to smallpox and other diseases

The first African slaves arrived in Cuba in 1513, but it wasn't until the late eighteenth century that the island's slave trade became a thriving enterprise. Africans were sold as slaves in public auctions. The last slave ship arrived in 1866, but it would take twenty more years before slavery was abolished there completely.

brought to the island by the Europeans. By 1570, the indigenous tribes on the island were completely wiped out. With no more Indians to use for labor, the European landowners imported African slaves to work the tobacco and sugarcane fields.

Because of its geographical location, Cuba was an important shipping port. The island's biggest settlement, Havana, was situated beside one of the country's many natural harbors on the north coast of the island. Pánfilo de Narváez, one of Velázquez's soldiers, founded Havana in 1514 and named it after a local Indian chief, San Cristóbal de Habana. The settlement was heavily fortified because it was regularly attacked by pirates.

In the late eighteenth century, some slaves in nearby Haiti revolted against the European colonists. French plantation owners gathered their slaves and fled to Santiago, where they established new sugarcane plantations. The industry grew rapidly, requiring more and more slave labor. It is estimated that 700,000 Africans were brought to Cuba in just forty years (1791 to 1830).

As France and Britain had already discovered, Spain found it increasingly difficult to keep their New World colonists happily under the government's control. The American and French Revolutions in 1776 and 1789, respectively, ignited calls for independence in Cuba as well. Ironically, the United States opposed Cuban independence, fearing blacks would become the ruling class and bring repercussions against the slave-owning southern states.

An Attack on a Galleon, by Howard Pyle, 1905

The fight for Cuban independence was led by José Martí, considered one of Cuba's greatest heroes and best poets. Born in Havana in 1853, Martí was exiled to Spain when he was seventeen years old for his vocal opposition to Spanish rule. While in Spain he published an exposé on the brutality of Cuban prisons based on his experience of being incarcerated in one.

During his exile, Martí traveled through Latin America and gained fame as a writer and poet with socially liberal views. He denounced the idea of social classes and believed that ignoring their existence would help eliminate them. Martí lived in New York City from 1881 to 1895. While there he organized the uprising that became the war for Cuban independence.

José Martí is one of Cuba's national heroes for his role in winning Cuba's independence. Statues honoring Martí can be found throughout the country, including in Cienfuegos, a city on the country's southern coast.

FYI FACT:

The revolt officially began in April 1895. Martí returned to Cuba and was killed in battle shortly thereafter, on May 19. The United States joined the war against Spain in February 1898, after the USS *Maine* was sunk in Havana Harbor. That December, Spain relinquished control of Cuba—but not to the Cuban people. The Treaty of Paris gave control of the island to the United States.

After Castro took power, it is estimated that two thirds of Cuba's doctors fled the island for the United States.

Many Cubans wanted to become a permanent part of the United States, but on May 20, 1902, Cuba was granted conditional independence: the U.S. reserved the right to intervene in Cuban affairs to preserve Cuba's independence from foreign powers.

In the years that followed, Cuba was a hotbed of rampant political corruption. A young lawyer named Fidel Castro believed a change in government was needed to improve the lives of Cubans. He particularly resented the rich Americans, whom he perceived controlled Cuba, and the American companies who owned and ran factories on the island.

Castro led a revolt that overthrew the democratic government and, by May 1961, had established Cuba as a socialist, or communist, state. He would rule the country for almost 50 years. During that time, Cuba became one of the most isolated countries on earth.

Fidel Castro

Cuba's terrain is varied, formed by earthquakes and volcanoes over the millennia. The eastern end of the island is mountainous, while the inner portion is filled with green, rolling plains. The southern part of the island is prone to tsunamis.

Cuba's unique location made it an important port of entry to the New World for European explorers and later settlers. It is perfectly situated to be a port of call, trading outpost, and shelter from the storms that frequently rage in the Caribbean.

The northern coast of the island touches both the Gulf of Mexico and the Atlantic Ocean. The southern coast faces the Caribbean Sea. The western tip of the island is only about 130 miles (209 km) from Cancún, Mexico. On the eastern end, the Windward Passage connects the Atlantic to the Caribbean and separates Cuba from Haiti.

The island is similar in shape to Tennessee—746 miles (1,200 km) long as the crow flies and between 22 and 130 miles (35 and 210 km) wide. Its coastline is filled with natural bays, coves, and inlets, so the actual perimeter winds over 3,500 miles (5,600 km). There are many marshes along the shoreline, and coral reefs and cays are plentiful. Because of its longstanding isolation and limited tourism, many areas of the island remain tropical paradises, boasting wide-ranging bio-diversity and well-preserved ecosystems.

The landscape ranges from semidesert to tropical rain forest. In general, the eastern end of the island is the most mountainous, with rugged cliffs overlooking the ocean. The interior of the island is hilly, with rolling plains and many limestone caverns. The southern part of the island is mostly flat and is frequently hit by hurricane-fueled tsunamis. The region is also prone to earthquakes because of the nearby Cayman Trench, located between Jamaica and Cuba.

Cuba is home to 90 species of lizards and 26 species of snakes, none of which are poisonous. The Cuban anole can grow to nearly two feet (54 centimeters) long.

The mountain ranges include the Cordillera de los Órganos to the west, the Sierra del Escambray in the central region, and the Sierra Maestra to the east. The highest range in Cuba, the Sierra Maestra is located in Santiago de Cuba Province, called Oriente Province since 1976, and its tallest peak, Turquino, stands over 6,500 feet (2,000 km) high. The range is mineral rich, holding iron, chromium, manganese, and copper deposits. It is also home to a diverse range of wildlife, including a butterfly with invisible wings that is found nowhere else on earth. Interestingly, there are no large predators in Cuba and no poisonous species of snakes.

The area has been geographically active for millennia, experiencing earthquakes and volcanic activity, so the topography of the sierra includes deep valleys and rugged terrain. These mountains have been a favored hiding place for rebels since the sixteenth century, when the Taíno Chief Hatuey led a losing revolt against the Spanish. Today, most of the Sierra Maestra remains wild and sparsely populated. It is a popular destination for hikers. Those who make it to the town of El

Cobre, nestled in a high valley within the range, can visit a well-known shrine to Cuba's patron saint, Our Lady of Charity.

Isla de la Juventud (Isle of Youth) is the second largest island in the Cuban archipelago and the sixth largest in the Antilles. Called the Island of Pines until 1978, it is located off the southwest coast of Cuba. The island has an estimated population of around 100,000 people. Nueva Gerona is the capital and largest city, while Santa Fe is the oldest.

Very little is known about the history of the island before Columbus arrived, but archaeologists have found some clues, such as hundreds of ancient cave drawings left by the original native population.

Columbus discovered the island during his first voyage to the New World in 1492. He originally named it *La Evangelista* (The Evangelist) and claimed it as a colony for Spain. It would undergo many name changes, variously called the Isle of Parrots and Treasure Island.

While Cuba has many lagoons, there are few true lakes. The only river big enough for navigation is the Rio Cauto in the southwestern part of the island. Although it is 230 miles (370 km) long, only 70 miles (113 km) is used as a commercial waterway. Even so, the island has many natural harbors that have enabled it to be an important port throughout its history.

Over three hundred species of birds make their home on the island. The Cuban trogon, commonly called the tocororo, is the national bird of Cuba. It feeds on flowers, insects, and fruit.

Cuba's semitropical climate is home to over 6,000 plant species. The east side of the island is covered with forests filled with over thirty species of palm trees as well as mahogany, cottonwood, cedar pine, and a variety of citrus trees. Mangrove swamps can be found along the southern coast.

There are only two mammals known to be indigenous to the island: the cane rat (*hutia*) and an insect-eating mammal called a solenodon, which looks like a giant shrew. Over three hundred species of birds make their home on the island, from wild turkeys and vultures to macaws and parakeets. The world's smallest bird, the bee hummingbird, or *zunzuncito*, is also found in Cuba. The tocororo is the national bird, selected for the honor because of its red, white, and blue feathers—the colors of the Cuban flag. Twenty-two percent of the country has been

The world's smallest bird is found in Cuba. The bee hummingbird, or *zunzuncito*, is around 2¼ inches long and weighs less than a tenth of an ounce. It's not much bigger than a bumblebee.

designated protected land, providing safe habitats for crocodiles, flamingos, orchids, and other wildlife.

There are more reptiles than any other land animal, including 15 types of snakes, none of them poisonous. In fact, the island does not have *any* plants or animals that are lethal to humans. However, there are some dangerous insects, such as the chigoe, a parasitic flea, and the Anopheles mosquito, which carries the malaria parasite.

The average annual temperature is 77°F (25°C), but during the summer it is frequently hot and very humid, although the northeasterly Trade Winds help temper the sticky heat. The rainy season lasts from May to October, and the island is frequently battered by hurricanes in the late summer and early fall.

FYI FACT:

In 1976, Cuba changed province boundaries, incorporating Holguín, Las Tunas, Guantánamo, Granma, and Santiago de Cuba into Oriente Province. The city of Santiago de Cuba is the capital of the new province.

Troubadours play music on a Santiago night.

Most Cubans live modestly in small homes, often with extended family members. Almost all Cuban teenagers attend boarding schools outside the city, where they have to do farm work in addition to their studies.

The People

Under European rule, after the indigenous population was effectively wiped out, those left alive on the island fell into three broad groups: colonists originally born in Spain, called *Peninsulari;* Creoles, colonists of European decent born on the island; and Africans imported as slaves. After the riots on Haiti, an influx of French colonists also settled in Cuba.

After England abolished slavery in 1832, and with slavery a hot-button political issue in the United States, the slave trade in Cuba was greatly diminished. Desperately needing workers for the sugarcane fields, plantation owners turned to China. In 1857, the first ship landed with Chinese workers. Twenty years later, the Chinese population was over 40,000.

Many of the Chinese workers married local Creoles and freed Africans—laws at the time prohibited them from marrying Spaniards. The Chinese Cubans developed a distinct culture and community, opening shops and restaurants. For a while in the early twentieth century, Havana's Chinatown was the largest in Latin America. By the time Fidel Castro came to power, the immigrant Chinese population on the island had been falling yearly, and it is estimated that under 500 immigrants born in China remain in Cuba today. Even though many Chinese Cubans left the island after the revolution that brought Castro to power, the Chinese influence on Cuban culture has become part of the fabric of the country. African influence is also visible throughout the island, especially in Cuban music and dance forms.

To honor the cultural contributions of the varied heritages that comprised Cuban nationality, in the 1890s, President José Martí decreed that there were no blacks or whites in Cuba, only Cubans. But the reality was, just as in the United States, blacks struggled as second-class citizens.

Despite living in a socialist country (which by definition is supposed to be egalitarian), Afro-Cubans have not achieved social equality, even though slightly over half the population of Cuba is of mixed African and European descent, called mulattos. Approximately 37 percent of Cubans are Caucasian; 11 percent black; and one percent Chinese. Cuba has 11 million residents, and nearly 30 percent of the populace lives in Havana.

Spanish is the official language of Cuba, although all students are required to study English in school. Catholicism is the main religion. Santería, a mystical religion that originated in West Africa, is also

The African cultural influence is apparent throughout Cuba. Afro-Cuban music is particularly popular and is played in many clubs. The rumba, tango, and mamba are traditional Cuban dances.

1 2 3 4 5 6 7 8 9 10 11 12 13 14 15 16 17 18 19 20

Cuban children start kindergarten as young as four years old. Cuba maintains the highest rate of literacy in Latin America. Education is free whether one attends a regular school or a specialized technical school.

practiced, and evangelical Protestant churches are becoming more popular.

When Castro came to power, he closed over 400 parochial (church-run) schools for spreading what he considered dangerous beliefs, and he declared the country an atheist state. But in 1991 the Cuban government lifted the prohibition against observing religion and the constitution was changed to identify Cuba as a secular state. There are still no parochial schools or Catholic-run hospitals. The Church isn't allowed to have Internet access, either. On the other hand, Christmas

Cuba is no longer an official atheist state, so citizens have the freedom to observe religion. As in the rest of Latin America, the primary religion is Catholicism.

was recognized as a holiday in 2007, for the first time in nearly 50 years. In addition to Christmas, the other national holidays are:

January 1	Liberation Day
January 2	Victory of Armed Forces
May 1	Labor Day
May 20	Independence Day
July 25-27	National Rebellion Memorial Days
October 10	Anniversary of the Beginning of the War of Independence in 1868

For all the religious restrictions still in place, and the monitoring of the Internet, secular education is highly valued in Cuba. The main colleges are the University of Havana, which was founded in 1728; the Universidad de Oriente in Santiago de Cuba; and Universidad Central de las Villas in Santa Clara.

Education is free to all Cuban citizens, whether they attend regular school or specialized technical schools. The school year starts in September and ends in June, and attendance is mandatory for children up to sixteen years old. The Cuban government claims the country has a 100 percent literacy rate, meaning every Cuban can read and write. As part of Cuba's commitment to literacy, there are a reported 1,000 libraries operating on the island, although most are under-funded.

Libraries are very community oriented in Cuba. They will deliver books to elderly or ill patrons. They also offer educational programs on the arts for children, and teach parents how to include reading into family time.

FYI FACT:

Chinese-Cuban cuisine is a blend of Caribbean and Chinese flavors and features many pork and rice dishes, such as Cuban Chinese fried rice.

The founder of the Ballet Nacional de Cuba, former prima ballerina Alicia Alonso has inspired dancers the world over. Although nearly blind, she continued to direct at the National Ballet well into her eighties. In 2002, Alonso was named UNESCO Goodwill Ambassador for her outstanding contribution to classical dance.

Culture and Lifestyle

Because they live in a communist state, Cubans are provided basic food, housing and utilities at a very low cost. Even so, average Cubans work hard to make ends meet—so they take their leisure time very seriously and make the most of it. The living quarters of most Cubans are small, so people enjoy being outside, especially for festivals and street fairs. International sporting events also take place in Cuba. The most popular sports are boxing, baseball, volleyball, and track and field.

Cubans have a deep appreciation for the arts, and the island hosts many regional and international cultural events. Castro's government strongly supported the arts, believing that artistic talent should be nurtured. There are many state-run fine art schools including the Cuban Film Institute, the National Council on Cultural Heritage, and the National School for the Arts. The international art world takes great interest in Cuba's artistic production.

Historically, writers have been especially revered in Cuba. After the revolution, however, Castro imposed censorship, meaning people were not allowed to write anything that was construed as critical of his government or promoted a different political system. But in the late 1980s some censorship provisions were eased, allowing more freedom of speech. The same is true for graphic arts. Censored for a long time, so-called "protest art" is permitted now, in part because it has become a very popular art form and brings significant revenue into Cuba.

The Cuban film industry has flourished under the Castros' regimes. Havana also hosts the New Latin American Film Festival every year, and movie tickets remain affordable. Since the film industry is run by the government, tickets are around fifteen cents, so watching films remains a favorite pastime. Similarly, it costs only about a quarter to attend the National Ballet of Cuba, because the dance company is supported by public funds to keep it accessible to all citizens.

Nothing expresses the Cuban culture more eloquently than dance and music. Cuban music is a melodic blend of styles and genres that date back to its colonial beginnings. Cuban music reflects its melting-pot heritage and the influences of Africa, Spain, France, the Southern United States, and Latin America. Afro-Cuban music is particularly popular and is performed publicly and privately everywhere in the country.

Son is another style of popular music that originated in the Oriente Province of Cuba. It is the foundation of modern salsa. A newer

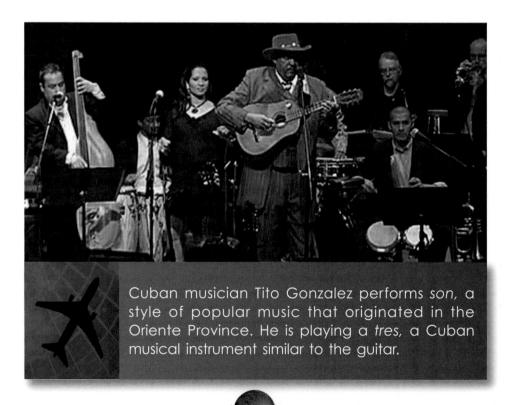

Cuban musician Tito Gonzalez performs *son*, a style of popular music that originated in the Oriente Province. He is playing a *tres*, a Cuban musical instrument similar to the guitar.

musical style is *timba,* which incorporates aspects of Brazilian music, hip-hop, and salsa. It has been described as salsa on steroids.

Cuban dance is equally rousing and is identified by sensual, fluid movements. Like the country's music, Cuban dance was informed by both the Spanish settlers and African slaves who came to the island. There are many types of Cuban dance styles, such as the rumba, which is a kind of Afro-Cuban dance. The rumba is usually accompanied by drums and the extensive use of maracas. The mamba is another popular dance derived from the rumba.

The tango may be closely associated with South America but its roots are in Cuba. The tango was derived from the habanera, a traditional Cuban dance. The conga can also trace its roots to Cuba. Tourists can go see examples of local dancing in any of the nightclubs now open in Havana and other major cities.

All that dancing can leave people hungry. Daily meals in Cuba are usually simple. The staples are rice, beans, fried plantains, vegetables, and pork in the form of *jamon vikin*, a type of ham. The biggest influence on Cuban cuisine is Spanish and African, with a sprinkle of Chinese. The traditional Cuban dish is called *Ajiaco Cubano,* a stew made with vegetable roots and pork. Other common Cuban dishes include *lechón asado en púa* (broiled pork cooked over an open fire), *tachinos* (fried unripe banana slices) or *tostones* (fried and mashed plantains), *frijoles negros dormidos* (black beans), and *tamales* (cornmeal filled with meat or corn).

FYI FACT:

Beef, which was once the most popular meat in Cuba, is now too expensive for the average Cuban to eat. Instead, pork and chicken have become the more affordable alternatives.

Ice cream is extremely popular in Cuba, as is cake, partly because both are considered special treats and only enjoyed on special occasions. Rum, on the other hand, is enjoyed frequently, and every club and restaurant offers an array of rum-based drinks, such as the minty Mojito.

For much of Cuba's history, sugarcane was its most important crop, although production has fallen in recent years. With the increasing global demand for biofuels, sugarcane could help Cuba become a world leader in the production of ethanol.

Chapter 6

Economy and Commerce

While Cuba's climate can create uncomfortable weather for people, the humidity and rain are very good for the country's main crops: sugar, rice, cassava (the root of which provides tapioca), and tobacco. Cuban cigars are prized the world over. The island is also the third largest producer of grapefruits in the world and has significant mineral reserves.

Sugarcane has been Cuba's primary crop for two hundred years and the majority of the available farmland was used to grow it. To diversify their agricultural output, in 2002 the Cuban government limited sugarcane crops to 60 percent of available land. The former sugar crop land was converted to vegetable farms and cattle ranches. Fishing is another important industry, and the Cuban commercial fishing fleet is one of the largest in Latin America. They sail from the tip of Argentina to the northern Atlantic.

In the 1970s and 1980s, the Soviet Union was Cuba's primary trading partner. During that time, the USSR was sending a million dollars a day in financial aid to Cuba. Life in Cuba became much more difficult after the breakup of the Soviet Union in the 1990s. Suddenly, countries that used to be part of the Soviet bloc were turning to democracy. While Russia adopted capitalism and a free market economy, Castro and his fellow Cubans reaffirmed their dedication to communism, making their country more isolated than ever. The country began struggling economically. Food was scarce and had to be rationed, along with hundreds of other goods such as clothes, medicine, and soap. The use of gasoline and oil was severely restricted. Factories cut back on work hours.

In 1993, over 50,000 Cubans suffered from severe vitamin B deficiency resulting in damage to the optic nerve which can cause loss of vision. The country ran out of chicken food so there were no fresh eggs to be found on the island. There were mandatory blackouts every day to try to conserve what fuel there was. Daily life became extremely hard and unless something changed, the country was headed for ruin. The situation was particularly hard on young people, who had grown up relying on the government. Even though nobody was rich, they had not lacked for things the way they did now.

Desperately needing revenue, Cuba turned to tourism. The government invested $3.5 billion during the 1990s to attract vacationers to the island. In 1994, the Ministry of Tourism was created. Most of the visitors were Canadian and European.

A bronze statue of John Lennon is found in a Havana Park that is named in honor of the former Beatle. In order to stop tourists from stealing the statue's glasses, the city posted a security guard (far right) to watch over the statue.

By 1995, tourism had become Cuba's top industry. By 2010, over two million tourists were visiting Cuba every year—including Americans who ignore the travel restrictions that are still in place. Risking hefty fines and even prison sentences, they get to the island on flights from Canada, Europe, or other countries. To encourage Americans, and American dollars, Cuban immigration officers don't stamp U.S. passports, helping violators avoid detection by U.S. officials. However, travel manifests—passenger lists for flights and cruises—may still be used to track travelers, and hundreds of U.S. tourists to Cuba are fined every year.

Technically, it is not illegal for Americans to go to Cuba. The Department of the Treasury issues special licenses that allow travel to the island. But they are generally restricted to journalists, Cuban-Americans with families still in Cuba, government officials, and people with religious or educational affiliations. The sanctions against American tourism to Cuba were put in place around 1960 in an effort to stop the flow of American dollars to Castro's communist regime.

Visitors to Cuba find a safe country—violent crime is extremely rare—that in many ways retains its Old World character while offering modern luxuries at well-tended hotels. With its rich history and abundant natural resources, Cuba has something to offer everyone.

FYI FACT:

Half the doctors and a majority of dentists in Cuba are women.

Until the revolution in 1959, the National Capitol building (*El Capitolio*) in Havana was the seat of the Cuban government. Today the building is home to the Cuban Academy of Sciences.

Chapter 7

Politics and Government

The political tension between poor workers and the wealthy minority has been a recurring theme in Cuba over the course of its history and ultimately resulted in Castro's rise to power. In the years after the Revolution, personal freedoms were severely curtailed but over time some of those restrictions have been lifted.

The Cuban Communist party (PCC) is the only legal political party. Legislative authority resides in the 609-member National Assembly of People's Power. The assembly members are elected by citizens but all candidates are selected by the Party.

This political system is called Democratic Centralism, the communist philosophy that government policy should be freely debated by members of the Party (hence, Democratic), but once the issue is decided by officials, all members of the parties are expected to obey their decision. In practical terms, it means the President has ultimate authority in Cuba, unlike in the United States where the president has limited authority, having to share it with Congress and the Supreme Court.

In 1976, Cuba adopted a constitution that established a system of representation called the Organs of People's Power (OPP), which are akin to U.S. city councils and county administrations. According to the Constitution, the OPP is supposed to be independent of the Cuban Communist Party, but in reality the Communist party selects candidates for OPPs at every governmental level. Technically, being appointed or elected to a government post does not require party membership, but in practice anyone who is not a party member is far less likely to be

Although he ruled Cuba for almost fifty years, not everyone supported Castro or his policies. According to a 2010 documentary on Castro called *He Who Must Live*, the former Cuban leader survived over 600 assassination attempts.

approved as a candidate for the local OPP and therefore cannot easily begin a political career.

The communist party is directed by its Central Committee, which is chosen every five years at a Party Congress—similar to U.S. political conventions. The First Secretary of the party chooses a smaller body of 25 persons called the Political Bureau that makes daily decisions.

When Fidel Castro was in power, he was President of the Republic as well as First Secretary of the PCC, President of the Councils of State and the Council of Ministers, and Commander in Chief of the Revolutionary Armed Forces (FAR). In other words, every decision had to meet his approval.

This is why Castro was frequently criticized and characterized as a dictator, and why the United States cut diplomatic ties with Cuba. In 1962, after Castro's government took ownership of American holdings in the country, the U.S. established a trade embargo that severely limits Americans from doing business in Cuba and restricts travel to the country. The Cuban embargo is the longest lasting between two countries in modern history.

On February 25, 2008, Fidel Castro officially stepped down as president of Cuba, and his brother Raúl was named president. Raúl promised to allow more free enterprise to help improve the economy. While many older Cubans still revere Castro, the younger generation welcomes the opportunity to earn more money and improve their standard of living.

Raúl also lifted the ban that prevented Cubans from patronizing hotels, restaurants, and other tourist destinations such as beaches. Allowing locals to mingle with foreign visitors was seen as another sign of reform. Raúl also announced in March 2008 that all Cubans could legally own cell phones and buy computers for the first time. Even though the country's poverty would keep such luxuries out of reach of most people, knowing the freedom is there is encouraging. Many political observers feel that Raúl may be more pragmatic than Fidel. He may also realize that in order for Cuba to economically survive and have the money to maintain the country's history and natural resources, it is imperative to integrate Cuba into the modern world.

FYI FACT:

The U.S. has had a military presence at Guantánamo since the late nineteenth century. Sometimes called the Pearl Harbor of the Atlantic, it is the oldest military base outside the U.S. and is approximately the size of Manhattan.

The official Cuban government photo of President Carlos Prío Socarrás, who served from 1948 to 1952. Suspected by some to have information regarding the assassination of U.S. President John F. Kennedy, Prío committed suicide in 1977.

Famous People

Cuban history is filled with colorful, passionate individuals who helped shape the island's history and its national identity.

Carlos Prío Socarrás

Carlos Prío Socarrás was the sixteenth and last constitutionally elected president of Cuba. Born in Bahia Honda, Cuba, on July 14, 1903, he became an anti-government activist while attending the University of Havana as a law student. He began his political career in 1940 when he was elected senator of Pinar del Rio province. In 1948, he was elected president.

Although he proved ineffectual at stopping the Mafia's growing influence in Cuba, under his presidency Cuba enjoyed more civil liberties and employment opportunities than it did before. It also remained a popular tourist destination for American and European tourists.

Before the scheduled presidential election in 1952, General Fulgencio Batista overthrew Prío's government. Prío fled Cuba for the United States. He settled in Miami where he worked as a real estate developer. His death from gunshot wounds on April 5, 1977, was ruled a suicide, but some conspiracy theorists believe he was killed because he had information about the Mafia's alleged involvement in President Kennedy's assassination.

Failing health forced Fidel Castro to step down as the acting president in 2008, turning leadership over to his brother Raúl. Since then, Raúl has eased many of the social restrictions put in place by Fidel in an attempt to modernize Cuba.

Fidel Castro

Castro began his professional life as a lawyer. The illegitimate son of a Creole sugar plantation owner, Castro was born in 1926 and was educated by Catholic Jesuit priests. When he was just thirteen, Castro helped organize a strike by the workers on his father's plantation.

He continued his activism as an adult. After becoming an attorney, he defended poor clients in Havana and was highly critical of the disparity of wealth in Cuba. He particularly resented the rich Americans he perceived controlled Cuba and the American companies who owned and ran factories on the island.

After Batista's 1952 overthrow of Prío's government, Castro decided the only way to gain reform was through revolution. He organized a group called the 26th of July Movement. Its goal was to overthrow Batista's government and rid Cuba of foreign influences such as the Mafia. Castro's followers waged a guerilla campaign against the government. They won and Castro effectively led Cuba for nearly fifty years until his brother Raúl took over in 2008.

Eduardo Chibás

Eduardo Chibás was a political activist who dreamed of a democratic Cuba. Born in 1907, Chibás was the son of a wealthy government engineer. He became politically active in his twenties and briefly joined a revolutionary group. He soon quit and adopted the radio as his weapon of choice against the government, using his Saturday-night broadcast to rally support from listeners.

Chibás formed his own political organization called the Cuban People's Party. He was generally opposed to communism and considered Prío's government corrupt and in the pocket of the Mafia. In 1951 Chibás emerged as the favorite to win the presidential election scheduled for June 1952.

But after it was revealed he mistakenly aired a false report of corruption, Chibás' popularity dropped. On August 5, 1951, Chibás shot

Eduardo Chibás (right)
and Ramon Grau

himself at the radio station. His plan was to kill himself while on the air, but because his speech ran so long, his mic had been turned off. He died on August 16 from his wounds.

Celia Cruz

Salsa singer Celia Cruz rose from local performer to international star but had to leave her homeland to do it. Born in Havana on Octo-ber 21, 1925, Úrsula Hilaria Celia de la Caridad Cruz Alfonso began singing on a popular local radio show contest. She won, taking home first prize: a cake. She continued performing in and winning singing contests and eventually was signed in 1948 to record her first album in Venezuela.

Her big break came when she joined the band Sonora Matancera as lead singer. Cruz toured with the band throughout the 1950s and

Born in Havana, Celia Cruz was one of the leading salsa singers in Latin America during the 1950s. Like many Cubans, after Castro came to power, Cruz relocated to the United States. She released over 70 albums in her career and appeared in ten movies, including *The Mambo Kings*.

became one of the top salsa singers in Latin America. In 1959 she was on tour with Sonora Matancera in Mexico when Castro rose to power. Rather than return to Cuba, Cruz and her musicians decided not to go back to Havana and went to the United States instead.

Cruz became an American citizen in 1962 and married Pedro Knight, who played trumpet in her band, and they settled in New Jersey. Cruz eventually achieved international fame as the Queen of Salsa and continued performing and recording up to her death in 2003.

Teófilo Stevenson

There have been many famous Cuban athletes but none more famous than Teófilo Stevenson, considered one of the greatest Olympic boxers in history. Stevenson was born in Camagüey in 1952. When he was thirteen he moved to Havana and began training as a boxer. When he was twenty, he competed at the 1972 Summer Olympics in Munich and won gold in the heavyweight division. He also won gold at the Montreal and Moscow summer games.

Considered one of the best heavyweight boxers in the world, he was offered millions of dollars to defect from Cuba and turn pro in the United States, since Castro outlawed professional sports. But Stevenson turned down the money and stayed in Cuba. He became vice president of the Cuban Boxing Federation and continues to be hailed a national hero.

Teófilo Stevenson (left)
vs. Olaf Walther, 1984

Festivals, parades, and street performances are very popular in Cuba. On most evenings, musicians and dancers can be found performing in cities from Santiago to Havana. The traditional dress reflects the African influence on Cuban artistic culture.

Festivals and Attractions

Whether it's dancing until dawn or communing with nature, Cuba offers a variety of attractions. For most people, the first stop is Havana, which has three distinct areas. The first is known as Old Havana. It is the oldest part of the city, where the original settlement was established and where many historical buildings stand. During the 1980s, in an effort to boost tourism and to instill a sense of pride in Cuban history, the government restored much of Old Havana.

The *Vedado,* or uptown district, is known for its shopping and nightlife. The third area is the more affluent suburbs to the west of the city, such as Miramar where diplomats and wealthy foreigners live. Several embassies are also located there.

In February, Havana hosts the annual Jazz Festival, which celebrates the connection between jazz and island rhythms that dates back to when newly freed Cuban slaves relocated to New Orleans. The festival began in 1979 as a local event but has grown into an international event.

Over 500 miles away from Havana is the second largest city, Santiago de Cuba, located on the southeast end of the island. An important cultural center, Santiago de Cuba has many museums and theaters but is especially known for being the home of many famous Cuban musicians. Like Havana, Santiago was built next to a bay and is a busy port city.

Filled with shady parks and lined by beautiful beaches, Santiago is considered one of the most picturesque areas of Cuba. In the summer,

Santiago de Cuba hosts two cultural festivals. The first, Fiesta del Fuego, is an eight-day celebration of Caribbean and Latin American culture. The streets are filled with live music and street performers and the celebrations last long into the nights. There are also parades filled with colorful floats. Then in August there is a music festival that features many live performances.

The political and cultural center of the city is Revolution Square, one of the largest plazas in the world, measuring 775,000 square feet. It is home to many government agencies as well as the National Library and statues and renderings of revered past Cuban politicians and revolutionaries.

In the late eighteenth century, French plantation owners fleeing from slave uprisings in Haiti relocated to Cuba and settled in Santiago, many with their slaves in tow. As a result, today Santiago is one of the most ethnically diverse cities in Cuba, the influences of both its European and African heritages visible throughout the city's culture.

A coffee plantation near Santiago de Cuba shows the Spanish architectural style present throughout the island. Santiago remains one of Cuba's most ethnically diverse cities.

Camagüey, the third largest city in Cuba, was attacked so frequently by pirates that the city was relocated from the northern coast to the center of the island in 1528. Although somewhat remote, Camagüey is easily reached by railroad. An hour's drive from the city is the beach resort of Santa Lucia, considered one of the most beautiful beaches in the Caribbean, with crystal-clear water, the world's second largest coral reef and colonies of pink flamingos. Novelist Ernest Hemingway was a frequent visitor to the area, where he enjoyed sailing and fishing.

The province of Holguín is the second most populous after Ciudad de la Habana, Havana's province. It is located in the southeast part of the island, and it is believed that this is where Columbus landed on October 28, 1492. He later described it as some of the most beautiful countryside he'd ever seen. The main industries in Holguín are beer brewing, agriculture (sugar and citrus), fishing and nickel mining. Every spring Holguín is the site of a large arts festival, *Romeriás de Mayo,* which attracts actors, musicians, dancers, writers, poets, and artists from all over the island to celebrate the Cuban arts.

Baracoa is still remote, so it retains a colonial, laid-back atmosphere. Near its small main square is the Assumption of the Virgin Mary Catholic Church, Cuba's first Catholic church, which houses the cross that Christopher Columbus brought ashore when he discovered the island. It is the oldest relic of Catholicism in the Americas. The city's most notable natural feature is El Yunque, a mountain that looks like an anvil. Visitors can hike to the top, passing through coffee and cacao plantations. There is live music every night at the Casa de la Trova, where locals gather to dance and relax. Baracoa is a five-hour car ride from Santiago, but those who take the time to visit will feel like they are stepping back into another world.

FYI FACT:

After Camagüey was attacked and burned by pirate Henry Morgan in 1668, the city was rebuilt with maze-like streets and alleys, making only one way out of the city. That way the people could trap any future pirates who tried to attack.

Cuba has some of the most beautiful coral reefs in the world. Valle de Coral Negro features coral walls more than 300 feet (100 meters) long. UNESCO has declared the coral reef at Maria la Gorda a biosphere reserve.

We Visit Cuba

Throughout Cuba there are many natural, social, and cultural places of interest to visit. One of the most spectacular historical sites is located on the southeastern corner of Isla de la Juventud, about 35 miles away from Nueva Gerona. The Cuevas de Punta del Este is a series of caves famous for over 200 pre-Columbian drawings found on their walls and ceilings. The caves were discovered in 1910 by a shipwrecked Frenchman. Archaeologists estimate the drawings were made around 800 CE by the Ciboney Indians. It is believed that the Ciboney civilization ended not long after the drawings were made. The most famous of the paintings has twenty-eight black and red concentric circles, which some experts have suggested represent a solar calendar.

Juventud is also known for its ecology. Not far from the caves is a beautiful beach popular with tourists. The underwater coral reefs, varied marine life, caves, and sunken ships attract many scuba enthusiasts. On land, La Jungla de Jones botanical garden has over 80 varieties of trees.

The most famous attraction on the island has a morbid past. The Presidio Modelo, or Model Prison, is located a few miles east of Nueva Gerona. This is where many political prisoners were held, including Fidel Castro before he successfully overthrew Cuba's government in 1959. There is a museum in the cell block where Castro was held, and visitors can view his former cell.

Santa Clara on the main island is a favorite destination for history buffs. The city features a monument to Che Guevara, a famous Cuban revolutionary. Throughout the country are many museums and other monuments that honor Cuba's fight for independence from Spain and eventual Castro-led revolution. In Trinidad, a town in the Sancti Spíritus province, for example, there is a museum devoted to the "bandits" of the 1959 revolution who fought in and around Trinidad. The museum is housed in the Iglesia y Convento de San Francisco, a former convent built by Franciscan monks in 1813. From the mid 1800s it was used as a church until it was converted into a jail.

Trinidad, which was founded in 1514 by Diego Velázquez, was a sugar center for many centuries and has been maintained better than many other Spanish-founded cities. The original colonial architecture can be seen in many places, with cobblestone streets and wrought iron gate works. Visitors can tour the city in horse-drawn carriages. Nearby is the Valley of the Sugar Mills, which has been declared a United Nations World Heritage site, where approximately seventy old sugar mills still stand.

FYI FACT:

Cuban crocodiles are known for their leaping ability. They can grow to 13 feet (4 meters) long and can weigh up to 300 pounds (135 kilograms).

Twelve miles from Trinidad is Topes de Collantes, a nature reserve that is a popular ecotourism spot. The reserve is a tropical rain forest that is home to many bird species, including the tocororo, over 40 orchid species, and 100 different kinds of ferns. Some of the ferns grow to over 20 feet (6 meters) tall. Forty species of coffee plants also grow there among the pine, mahogany, eucalyptus, and magnolia trees.

In Matanzas province, about 100 miles (160 km) south of Havana, is Zapata Swamp—officially called the Ciénaga de Zapata Biosphere Reserve—a national park known for its crocodile nursery, dedicated to restoring the Cuban crocodile population on the island. Visitors can tour the facility, where young crocodiles are raised at the nursery and tended to by veterinarians. They are released into the wild when they are old enough to survive on their own.

Havana offers a different kind of tourist experience. Although a modern city in many ways, it is filled with reminders of Cuba's past. Three different forts—the Castillo de la Real Fuerza, one of the oldest in the Americas; Castillo del Morro; and San Salvador de la Punta— were built to protect Havana from pirates. The pirates are long gone, but the forts and city walls still guard the entrance to Havana Bay, a reminder of the island's precarious past.

Castillo de la Real
Fuerza

Tostones

Plantains are a staple of Cuban cuisine, and *tostones,* also known as *tachinos* in some parts of the country, are very popular and very easy to make. Just make sure you try this recipe with an adult present.

Ingredients
2 green plantains
Oil for frying
Salt

To prepare
Ask an adult to heat about ½ inch of oil in a heavy skillet over medium-high flame.
While the oil is heating, peel the green plantains and then cut them into ¾-inch slices.
Fry the slices in the hot oil for 3 minutes, until they are a light golden color and somewhat soft (not mushy).
Use a slotted spoon to remove the plantain slices. Place them on paper towels to drain. Let them cool for about a minute.
Smash the plantains into flat rounds.
Fry the rounds in the hot oil for 3 minutes, until they are crisp and golden brown.
Use a slotted spoon to remove the *tostones.* Place them on paper towels to drain.

You can serve the *tostones* with just some salt to taste, or with garlic dip.

Sugar Bowl

You can paint a sugar bowl to reflect Cuba's sugar industry. Paint the lid bright red—one of the main colors on the Cuban flag. Add sugarcanes and stars, also from the flag. *Azúcar* means "sugar."

You'll need:
small clay flower pot
clay saucer that fits into the top
1-inch wooden ball
glue
small sponge
1½-inch wooden disks
black, white, yellow, red, blue, brown paints
several paintbrushes

1. Wash and dry the pot and saucer. Glue a wooden disk in the bottom of the pot to cover the hole. Glue the wooden ball to the bottom of the saucer.
2. Paint the lid and wooden ball red. Paint the pot blue using a separate brush. Let them dry.
3. Dab a small amount of white paint with the corner of the sponge, then sponge clouds into the blue sky on the pot.
4. Paint the sugarcanes brown. Use a brush to mix a little white with brown to add texture.
5. Paint the letters black using a separate brush.
6. Add some yellow stars—or paint them whatever color you wish.
7. Clean your brushes carefully with soap and water. Allow your painted pot to air dry for 7 days before hand washing it.

1514 Diego Velázquez designates Santiago de Cuba a Spanish colony; Pánfilo de Narváez founds Havana

1763 The Treaty of Paris returns Cuba to Spain

1868 War of independence begins

1895 Second war of independence led by Cuban nationalist José Martí

1898 Spain relinquishes all claims to Cuba after military defeat by the United States

1902 Cuba swears in its first independent president, Tomás Estrada Palma

1906 President Tomás Estrada Palma resigns; the United States invades Cuba

1924 Gerardo Machado becomes president

1933 Machado is overthrown in a coup

1952 General Fulgencio Batista seizes power of Cuba and establishes a brutal regime

1956 Castro begins a guerrilla war against the Batista government

1958 The U.S. stops military aid to General Batista

1959 Castro's army overthrows Batista; Castro becomes prime minister

1960 Cuba takes control of all U.S.-owned businesses in Cuba

1961 The U.S. and Cuba sever diplomatic relations; an invasion by Cuban exiles at the Bay of Pigs fails; Castro declares Cuba a socialist state

1962 The Cuban Missile Crisis brings the world to the brink of nuclear war

1976 A new socialist constitution is approved

1980 More than 100,000 Cubans flee to the U.S.

1991 Soviet military advisers leave Cuba following the collapse of the USSR

1998 Pope John Paul II visits Cuba

2008 Castro, suffering from ill health, announces his resignation in February

2009 U.S. President Barack Obama lifts travel sanctions against Cuban-Americans who want to visit relatives in Cuba

2010 A first in U.S.-Cuba relations, Director of Deposito del Automovil (the Cuban Automotive Museum) Ing. Eduardo Mesejo Maestre becomes the first Cuban official to judge a major U.S. automotive Concours

Books

Engle, Margarita, and Sean Qualls (illustrator). *The Poet Slave of Cuba: A Biography of Juan Francisco Manzano.* New York: Henry Holt and Co., 2006.

Francis, Amy. *The U.S. Policy on Cuba.* Farmington Hills, MI: Greenhaven Press, 2009.

Green, Jen. *National Geographic Countries of the World: Cuba.* Washington, D.C.: National Geographic Children's Books, 2007.

Hughes, Susan. *Cuba: The People.* New York: Crabtree Publishing Company, 2004.

Petersen, Christine, and David Petersen. *Cuba.* New York: Children's Press, 2002.

Works Consulted

Anderson, Jon Lee. *Che Guevara: A Revolutionary Life.* New York: Grove Press, 1997.

Baker, Christopher. *Mi Moto Fidel: Motorcycling Through Castro's Cuba.* Washington, D.C.: National Geographic, 2001.

Bethell, Leslie. *Cuba: A Short History.* New York: Cambridge University Press, 1993.

DePalma, Anthony. "History Lessons on Cuba for a New President." *New York Times,* January 3, 2009. http://www.nytimes.com/2009/01/04/weekinreview/04DePalma.html

Gott, Richard. *Cuba: A New History.* New Haven, CT: Yale University Press, 2004.

Kapcia, Antonio. *Cuba: Island of Dreams.* Oxford: Berg, 2000.

Miller, Tom (editor). *Travelers' Tales Cuba: True Stories.* Palo Alto, CA: Travelers' Tales, 2001.

Olmsted, Victor H., and Henry Gannett. *Cuba: Population, History and Resources 1907.* Washington, D.C.: United States Bureau of the Census, 1909.

Rangel, Carlos. *The Latin Americans: Their Love-Hate Relationship with the United States.* New York: Harcourt Brace Jovanovich, 2005.

Thomas, Hugh. *Cuba or the Pursuit of Freedom.* Cambridge, MA: Da Capo Press, 1998.

On the Internet

Council of Hemispheric Affairs. "A Constructive Plot to Return Guantánamo Bay to Cuba in the Near Future." March 15, 2007. http://www.coha.org/2007/03/a-constructive-plot-to-return-guantanamo-bay-to-cuba-in-the-near-future/

Dorfman, Ariel. Time 100: "Che Guevera." *Time,* n.d. http://205.188.238.109/time/time100/heroes/profile/guevara01.html

Global Security: Cuban History http://www.globalsecurity.org/military/world/cuba/history.htm

History of Cuba http://www.historyofcuba.com/cuba.htm

Hunt, Nigel. History of Cuban Nation http://www.cubahistory.org/

Kids' Guide to Cuba http://www.cubacuban.com/kids/index.shtml

Making Music: Music of Cuba http://www.sbgmusic.com/html/teacher/reference/cultures/cuba.html

Schweimler, Daniel. "Che's Spirit Burns On in Latin America." *BBC News,* January 3, 2009. http://news.bbc.co.uk/2/hi/americas/7785690.stm

Wilkinson, Jerry. "History of Cuba." Historical Preservation Society of the Upper Keys. http://www.keyshistory.org/cuba.html

GLOSSARY

Antilles (an-TIL-eez)—Another name for the Caribbean islands.

archipelago (ar-kih-PEH-luh-goh)—A chain or cluster of small islands.

art deco (art DEH-koh)—An architectural style that gained popularity in the 1920s, characterized by geometric designs and bold colors.

cassava (kah-SAH-vuh)—A starchy root plant that is the source of tapioca.

cavern (KAA-vern)—A large cave.

cay (KAY)—A small island or reef made of coral or sand.

conquistador (kon-KEY-stuh-door)—A sixteenth-century Spanish soldier who explored Mexico and other parts of the New World for Spain and claimed the area for the Spanish monarchy.

coup (KOO)—The overthrow of a government through military force.

Creole (KREE-ohl)—A person of European descent born in the West Indies or in Latin America.

Freeman (FREE-man)—A person who is not enslaved; someone who has all civil liberties.

guerrilla (gur-IL-uh)—A person who fights in unconventional warfare, using such tactics as small group deployment, raids, and ambushes.

infamous (IN-fuh-mus)—Having a bad reputation; known for committing unlawful acts.

lagoon (lah-GOON)—A body of water separated from a larger body of water by a coral reef or sandbar.

Peninsulare (pay-NIN-soo-lar-ay)—A Cuban colonist or resident who was born in Spain.

secular (SEH-kyoo-lur)—Nonreligious.

totalitarian (toh-tal-uh-TAYR-ee-un)—A form of government that strictly controls the actions of its citizens.

Trade Winds—Winds that blow continuously in one direction, especially the easterly winds near the earth's equator.

INDEX

Kathleen Tracy has been a journalist for over twenty years. Her writing has been featured in magazines including *The Toronto Star*'s "Star Week," *A&E Biography* magazine, *KidScreen*, and *TV Times*. She is also the author of numerous books for Mitchell Lane Publishers, including *The Fall of the Berlin Wall; Paul Cézanne; The Story of September 11, 2001; The Clinton View; Johnny Depp; Mariah Carey;* and *Kelly Clarkson.* Tracy lives in the Los Angeles area with her two dogs and African Grey parrot.